Positive Affirmations For Kids

Inspired by

Jayden F. Nyiawung
and
Taliyah M. Nyiawung

Hello _________________________,

You have the power to achieve anything.
What ever you do, do it with love.
Trust in yourself.

I AM UNIQUE

1

I am unique

I am happy to be different.
I am one of a kind.
My character makes me valuable.
I am wonderful just as I am.
I am proud of myself.

Why are you special?

I AM AWESOME

I am awesome

I am loved and valued for who I am.

I am worthy of wonderful things. I am smart and talented.

I am a shining star.

I can light up the world.

I feel good!

What other things make you so awesome?

I AM FULL OF LOVE

I am full of love

I am loved and valued.
I am full of kindness.
I am filled with love.
I share love with those around me.
I love myself just as I love others.

Why do you love yourself ?

I AM HEALTHY

I am healthy

I love and respect my body.
I eat healthy foods to nourish my body.
I enjoy being active.
I spend time in nature.
I practice being still and silent every day.
I am healthy and happy.

What other things do you do to stay healthy?

I AM HAVING FUN

I am having fun

I am playful and love to have fun.
I laugh and smile every day.
I have fun learning and creating!
I enjoy trying new things.
I am having fun.

What other things do you do to have fun?

I AM GRATEFUL

11

I am grateful

I am grateful for my life.
I am grateful for my family and
friends.
I am thankful for my teachers and
 guardians.
I am thankful for my community.
I am thankful for all the love in my
life.

What else are you grateful for?

13

I am kind

I love helping others.
I treat others the way I want to be treated.
I am patient with myself and others.
I am a good listener.
I show love through kind words and actions.

How will you show kindness to others?

I TAKE CARE OF MY BODY

15

I take care of my body

I appreciate my body.
I practice good hygiene to keep myself healthy.
I drink plenty of water every day.
I get enough rest and sleep to help my body heal.

How do you care for your body ?

I AM HONEST

17

I am honest

I am honest with myself and others.
I am truthful even when nobody is watching.
I take responsibility for my actions.
I admit my mistakes and learn from them.
I am proud of myself when I am honest, even in difficult situations.
I am trusted when I am honest.

Why is it good to be honesty?

I AM BRAVE

I am brave

I face my fears with courage.
I believe in myself and my abilities.
I stand up for myself and what I
believe.
I am powerful to try new things.
I am brave and strong.

Why should you be brave?

I AM CREATIVE

21

I am creative

I am free to express myself creatively.
I am full of great ideas and thought.
I have the power to create anything I desire.
I use the opinion of others for my growth.
My creativity is a gift that I love to share with the world.
I have unique abilities and talents.

Why is it good to be creative?

I AM DISCIPLINED

23

I am disciplined

I am willing and excited to learn.
I am disciplined and focused in all I do.
I am in control of my actions and choices. I am in a competition with myself.
I take responsibility for my actions.

What are the benefits of being disciplined?

I AM HAPPY

I am happy

I am happy to be alive.
I deserve to be happy.
I deserve good things in my life.
I appreciate the beauty of the world.
I am blessed!

Why is it good to be happy?

I LOVE TO FORGIVE

27

I love to forgive

I forgive myself and everyone.
I let go of all that makes me unhappy.
I fill myself with love by forgiving others.
I pray for myself and others.
I am peaceful and happier when I forgive.

How do you feel when you forgive?

I AM CONFIDENT TO SHARE HOW I FEEL

I am confident to share how I feel

I am comfortable sharing how I feel.
I am capable of expressing my emotions in healthy ways.
Expressing my feelings is a sign of strength .
I express my feelings positively.
I am proud of myself.

How are you feeling today?

I am blessed !
I am special!
I can be anything I want!